POWER THOUGHTS

POWER THOUGHTS

365 Daily Affirmations

Louise Hay

HAY HOUSE, INC.
Carlsbad, California ▸ New York City
London ▸ Sydney ▸ Johannesburg
Vancouver ▸ Hong Kong ▸ New Delhi

Published and distributed in the United States by: Hay House, Inc.:
www.hayhouse.com • *Published and distributed in Australia by:* Hay House Australia
Pty. Ltd.: www.hayhouse.com.au • *Published and distributed in the United Kingdom
by:* Hay House UK, Ltd.: www.hayhouse.co.uk • *Published and distributed in the
Republic of South Africa by:* Hay House SA (Pty), Ltd.: www.hayhouse.co.za • *Distributed
in Canada by:* Raincoast Books: www.raincoast.com • *Published in India by:* Hay House
Publishers India: www.hayhouse.co.in

Editorial supervision: Jill Kramer • *Design:* Jenny Richards • *Illustrations:* Digital Stock

Library of Congress Control Number: 2004109885

ISBN 13: 978-1-4019-0554-5
ISBN 10: 1-4019-0554-4

18 17 16 15   14 13 12 11
1st printing, June 2005

Printed in China

Dedicated to all of us who want life to be easy. Changing our lives for the better does not have to be difficult work. Thinking one or two new, powerful, positive thoughts a day is the way.
One day at a time . . .
and life becomes sublime.

Introduction

This little book is filled with positive affirmations. Every thought you think and every word you speak is an affirmation. So why not choose to use only positive affirmations to create a new and fulfilling life? Day by day you'll find new ideas for how to make each day a delightful experience.

An affirmation is like planting a seed. You're always in the process of tending to your garden, and if you do so with care, you'll find that each day becomes more joyous than the one before it.

You have the power and authority to take control of your thoughts and your life. By reading these affirmations—one a day, several at a time, or just by opening the book at random—you're taking the first step toward building a more rewarding life.

I know you can do it!

— Louise Hay

1

I choose to feel good about myself each day. **Every** morning I remind myself that I can make the choice to feel good. This is a new habit for me to cultivate.

2

I am always
presented
with new and
wonderful
opportunities.
I flow with
what is
happening in
the moment.

3

I now accept
and appreciate
the abundant
life the
Universe
offers me.

4

Love is
the miracle
cure. Loving
myself works
miracles in
my life.

5

Changes can begin in this moment. I am willing to change.

6

I am pleased with all that I do. I am good enough just as I am.

7

It is my birthright to live fully and freely.

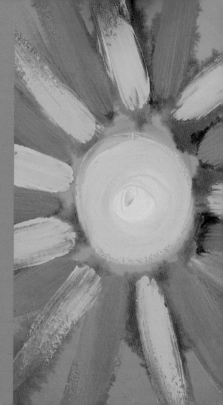

8

I allow my
income to
constantly
expand, and
I always live
in comfort
and joy.

9

I recognize my body as a good friend.

10

I am the
creative
power in
my world.
I express
myself
creatively as
much as
possible.

11

Good now
flows into my
life from
expected and
unexpected
channels.

12

My heart is open. I am willing to release all resistance.

13

I have the
perfect living
space. It is
safe, and
filled with
loving
thoughts.

14

I am one with
the power and
wisdom of the
Universe. I
have all that
I need.

15

I am
unlimited
in my own
ability to
create the
good in
my life.

16

I breathe
freely and
fully. Breath
is the basis
of life.

17

I have many
dreams, and
I know that
I deserve to
have these
dreams
come true.

18
My joyful
thoughts
create my
joyful world.

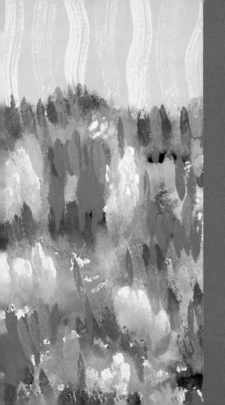

19
I have
my own set
of talents
and abilities.

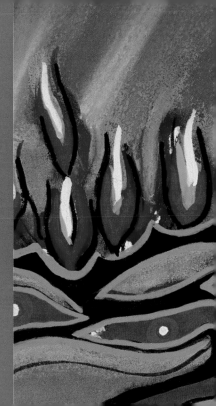

20

I now release anger in positive ways. I love and appreci- ate myself.

21

I keep my
thoughts
centered on
what I wish
to experience.

22

I am equally
blessed with
love, harmony,
and joy.
I take in life
in perfect
balance.

23

The Ocean
of Life is
lavish with
its abundance.
Golden oppor-
tunities are
everywhere.

24

I see clearly.
I now create
a life I love to
look at.

25

I allow my
love to flow
freely. My
supply of love
is endless.

26

I feed my body nourishing foods and beverages, and I exercise in ways that are fun.

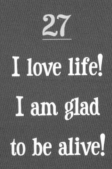

27
I love life!
I am glad
to be alive!

28

I am willing to release the need to be unworthy. I am now becoming all that I am destined to be.

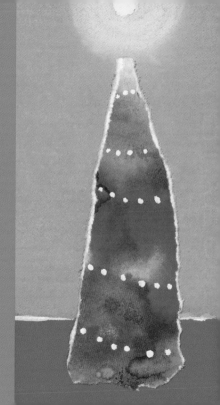

29

I feel good about everyone I meet. All my relationships are healthy and nourishing.

30

I forgive
myself and
set myself
free.

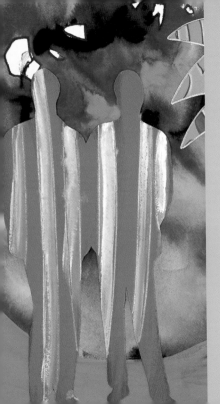

31

I feel
tolerance,
compassion,
and love for
all people,
myself
included.

32

It is safe for me to go beyond my parents' limitations. I am free to be me.

33

I only speak
words that
are loving,
positive, and
constructive.

34

I release all
struggle now,
and I am
at peace.

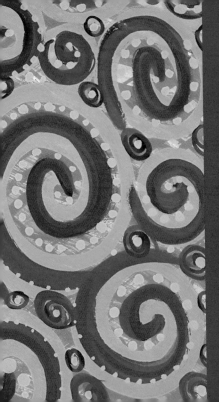

35

Life created me to be fulfilled. I now release all expectations, and I know that I am taken care of.

36

No person,
place, or
thing has any
power over
me, for I am
the only
thinker in
my mind.

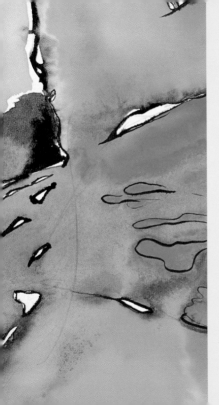

37

Every
experience I
have benefits
me. I am in
the process
of positive
change.

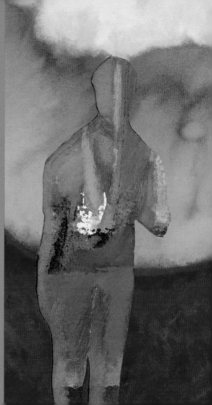

38

My body
represents
perfection.
I am
vibrantly
healthy.

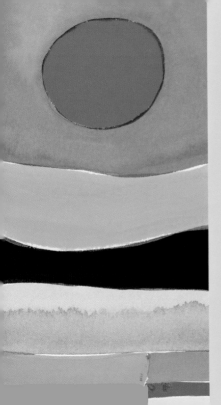

39

I rise
above all
limitations. I
am **Divinely**
guided and
inspired.

40

I am mentally and emotionally equipped to enjoy a loving, prosperous life. I am deeply fulfilled by all that I do.

41

I am
joyous today.
Humor
and fun
contribute to
my total
well-being.

42

Life brings
me only good
experiences.
I am open to
new and
wonderful
changes.

43

I am always
able to make
the correct
decision. I
recognize my
own intuitive
ability.

44

My heart is opening wider and wider. Love flows *from* me and *to* me in ever-increasing amounts. I feel great. People love being around me.

45

I rejoice
in others'
successes,
knowing that
there is
plenty for
us all.

46

Miracle follows miracle in my life. I accept miraculous occurrences in my life and in my world.

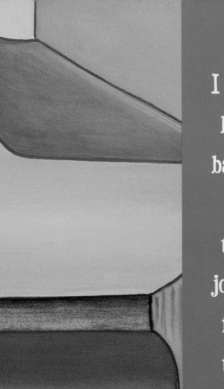

47

I release any
limitations
based on old,
negative
thoughts. I
joyfully look
forward to
the future.

48

I always have
wonderful,
harmonious
relationships.
The person
I am looking
for is now
looking for me.

49

Within
myself I see
a loving,
beautiful
being. It is
safe for me to
look within.

50

My life continues to get better and better. I now move into my greater good.

51

I am the president of my own world, and I act with honor and integrity in all that I do.

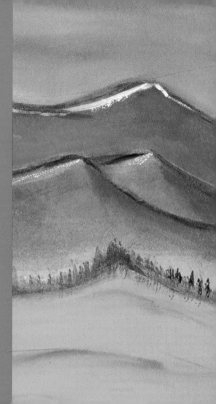

52

We are all
family, and
the planet is
our home.

53

I focus on
positive
thoughts
because the
thoughts I
think and the
words I speak
create my
experiences.

54

I am
joyously
exuberant and
in harmony
with all
of life.

55

I now choose
to release
every negative,
destructive,
fearful idea
and thought
from my mind
and my life.

56

I use my
power wisely.
I am strong,
and I am safe.
All is well.

57

Life supports
me every step
of the way.
I am fed,
clothed, housed,
and loved in
ways that are
deeply fulfill-
ing to me.

58

I am worth loving. There is love all around me.

59

I radiate
health,
happiness,
prosperity,
and peace
of mind.

60

I move
beyond old
limitations
and now
express myself
freely and
creatively.

61

I trust my
Higher Self.
I listen with
love to my
inner voice.

62

I open myself to the wisdom within, knowing that there is only One Intelligence in this Universe.

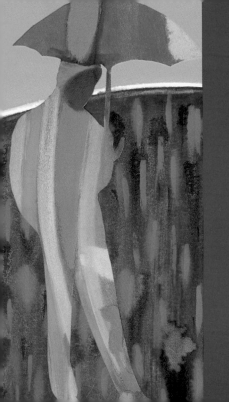

63

When I
listen to my
inner self,
I find the
answers
I need.

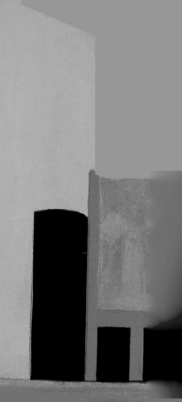

64

It is healing
to show my
emotions.
It is safe for
me to be
vulnerable.

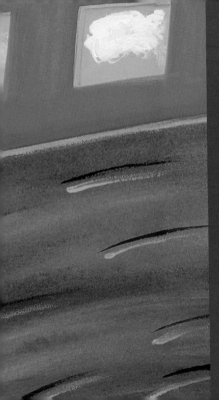

65

I open my
consciousness
to all the
wonderful
possibilities
of life.

66

I am safe
in the
world. I am
comfortable
with change
and growth.

67

Whatever
I need to
know is
revealed to me
at exactly the
right time.

68

I see
myself as a
magnificent
being who is
wise and
beautiful. I
love what I
see in me.

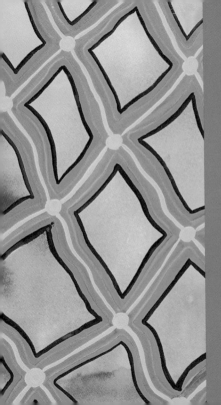

69

I recognize
my body as a
wondrous
machine,
and I feel
privileged to
live in it.

70

When I really love myself, everything in my life works.

71

I am
in charge.
I take my
own power
back.

72

I am good
enough
just as I am.
I approve of
myself at
all times.

73

I relax, and
recognize my
self-worth.

74

I travel safely
wherever I
go. I always
meet loving,
helpful people
on my
journey.

75

I give myself
the green
light to go
ahead, and
to joyously
embrace
the new.

76

The people in my life are really mirrors of me. My world is safe and friendly.

77

Today is my
stepping-stone
to new
awareness
and greater
glory.

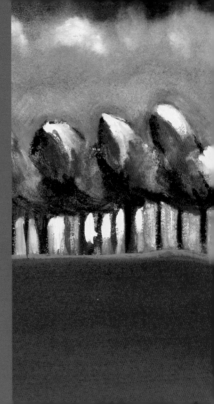

78

Freedom and
change are
in the air. I
discard old
ideas.

79

I am good
enough. Life
is easy and
joyful.

80

My body
takes me
everywhere,
easily and
effortlessly.

81

I surround
myself with
loving people
who only see
the good
in me.

82

I breathe life
into my
vision and
create the
world I
desire.

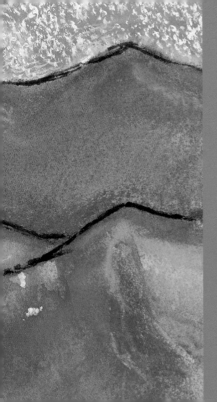

83

My life is
joyously
balanced
with work
and play.

84

Divine
Intelligence
gives me
all the ideas
I can use.

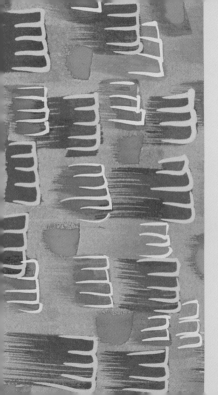

85

I feel reborn.
I am free
from the past,
and I joyously
welcome
the new.

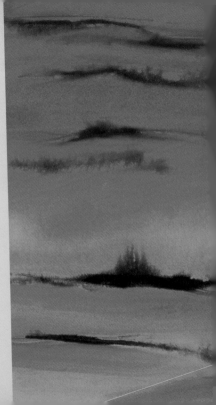

86

I see the best
in everyone
and help
them bring
out their
most joyous
qualities.

87

I have compassion for my parents' childhoods. I now know I chose them because they were perfect for what I had to experience and understand.

 88

I am created
to succeed,
and I
now give
thanks for
my success.

89

The more I help others, the more I prosper and grow. In my world, everybody wins.

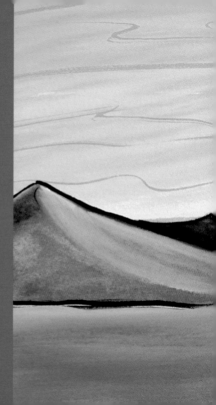

90

I am always
on time,
which is a
way of
showing
respect to
those in
my life.

91

I speak
up for myself.
I claim my
power now.

I love myself
exactly the
way I am.

93

I am able to
freely express
my emotions
at all times.

94

My body
mirrors my
state of mind.
I am healthy,
whole, and
complete.

95

I keep my thoughts positive. Life brings me the good experiences I deserve.

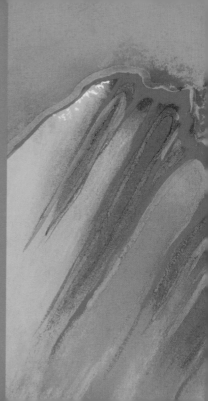

96

I am
unlimited in
my ability to
create good
in my life.

97

I am lovable

because I

exist.

My uniquely creative talents and abilities flow through me and are expressed in deeply satisfying ways.

99

I am safe
where I am.
I create my
own security.

100

I am in the
right place
at the
right time,
doing the
right thing.

101

Every
experience in
my life is an
opportunity
for growth.

102

I allow the love from my heart to wash through me and cleanse and heal every part of my body and emotions.

103

I am grateful
to others for
the kindness
they show
me. I am
filled with
praise
and gratitude.

104

I open my consciousness to the expansion of life. There is plenty of space for me to grow and change.

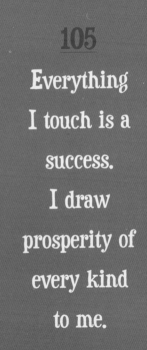

105

Everything
I touch is a
success.
I draw
prosperity of
every kind
to me.

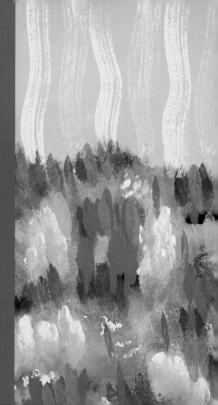

106

All my relationships are harmonious. I see only harmony around me at all times.

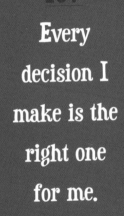

107

Every decision I make is the right one for me.

108

I love who
I am and
what I do.

The past is
over and
cannot be
changed. This
is the only
moment I can
experience.

110

I am at peace with the elements of nature. There is no "good" or "bad" weather. I can choose my individual reaction to it.

111

I stand in
truth and live
and move
in joy.

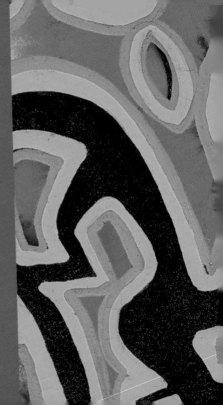

112

I create miracles in my wonderful world. I am open to the wonders of the Universe.

113

I trust
myself, and I
trust Life to
support and
protect me.

114

I earn an excellent income doing what satisfies me. I know I can be as successful as I make up my mind to be.

115

I am willing
to see how
and where I
need
to change.

116

Today I do a mental housecleaning, making room for new, positive thoughts.

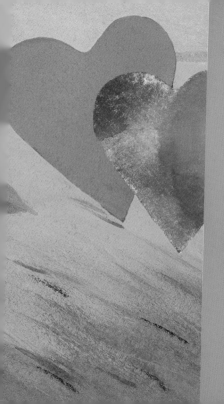

117

I am a
Divine,
magnificent
expression
of life. Love
surrounds
and protects
me.

118

I release
the need to
blame anyone,
including
myself.

119

I am one
with the very
Power that
created me.

120

I give
thanks for
everything
that is
lovingly
supplied
to me.

121

I now take
care of
my body,
my mind,
and my
emotions.
I feel good!

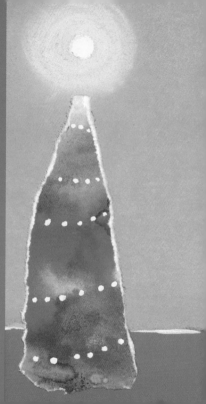

122

I constantly find new ways of looking at my world. I see beauty everywhere.

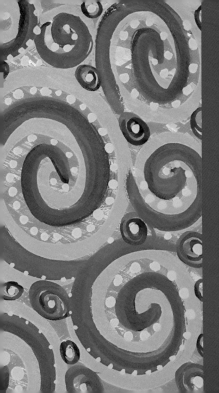

123

I bless and prosper others, and they, in turn, bless and prosper me.

124

I envision a
world of peace
and plenty.
I feel harmony
and unity
between
nations, and I
contribute to
that harmony.

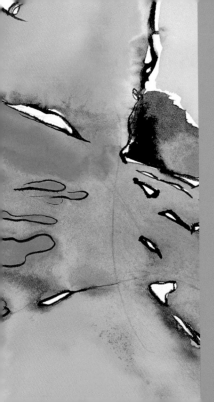

125

There is
enough time
and space for
everything I
want to do.

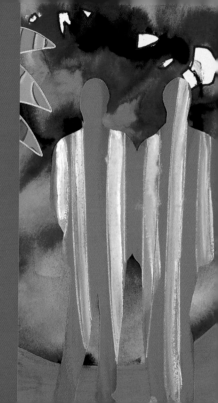

126

Loving people fill my life, and I find myself easily expressing love to others.

127

I express
gratitude to
my own
mother, and
to all the
mothers in the
world who
give their
children love.

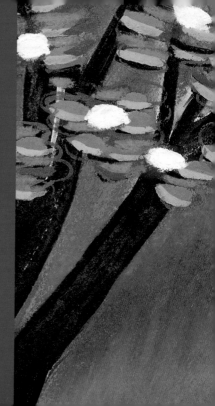

128

I love my
family and
my home. I
feel nurtured,
warm,
and safe.

129

I trust
life to be
wonderful.
I see only
good ahead
of me.

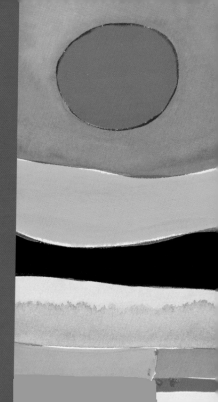

130

I open my consciousness to the expansion of life. There is plenty of space for me to grow and change.

131

I give to Life
exactly what
I want Life to
give to me.

132

I say, "Out!" to every negative thought that comes into my mind.

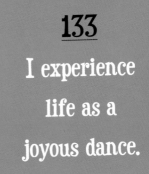

133

I experience
life as a
joyous dance.

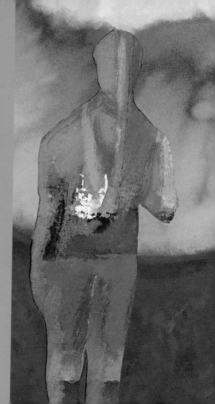

134

My body
is ideal for
me in this
lifetime.

135

I release the pattern of procrastination within me. I act with speed and resolve.

136

I look terrific
and feel
terrific.
Here I am,
world—
open and
receptive
to all good!

137

I release any
feelings of
competition or
comparison. I
simply do my
best and enjoy
being me.

138

All that I
need to know
at any given
moment is
revealed
to me. My
intuition is
always on
my side.

139

I ask for
what I want.
I know that
whatever
I need will
always be
there for me.

140

I trust in the Power that created me to protect me at all times and under all circumstances.

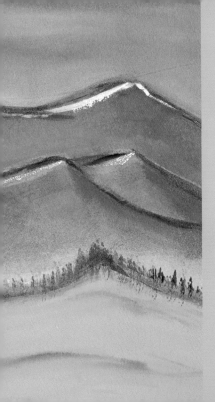

141

I joyfully help wherever I can, easing the load of others.

I rise above
all limita-
tions. I am
Divinely
guided and
inspired.

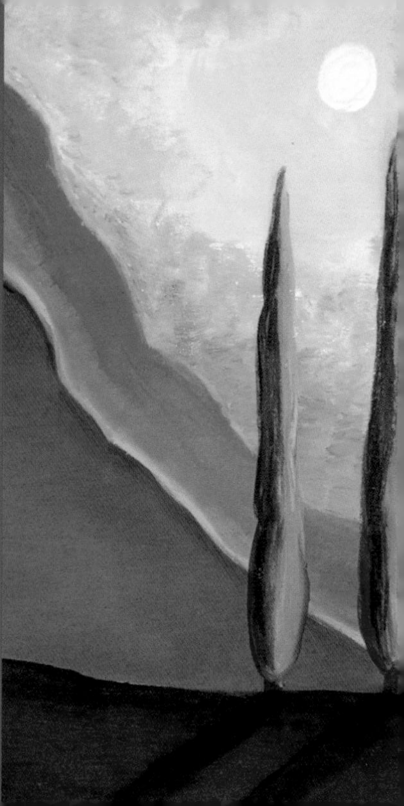

143

I am
special and
wonderful.
The more
I love myself,
the less stress
I have.

144

I am patient,
tolerant, and
diplomatic.

145

I expect my
life to be good
and joyous,
and it is.

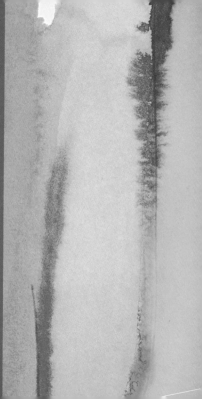

146

I ask for more
understanding
so that I may
knowingly
and lovingly
shape my
world
and my
experiences.

147

I see
abundance
radiating all
around me.
I now live in
limitless love,
light, and joy.

148

**Every change
in my life
can lift me
to a new
level of
understanding.**

149

I create new memories filled with peace, good-will, and compassion for others.

150

When I find harmony and balance in my mind, I find it in my life.

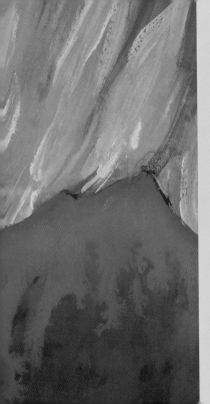

151

I now choose to recognize the magnificence of my being.

152

I respect
others for
being
different, but
not wrong.
We are
all one.

153

I am led to fulfilling experiences. I create a life filled with rewards.

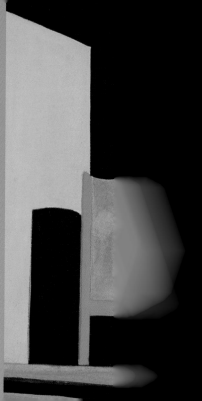

154

I am very well organized. Life is simple and easy.

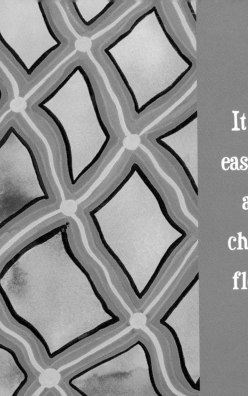

155

It is always easy for me to adapt and change. I am flexible and flowing.

156

What I give
out, I get back.
I give out only
goodness and,
in turn, only
goodness
comes back
to me.

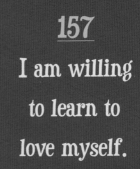

<u>157</u>

I am willing
to learn to
love myself.

158

I break new
ground and
begin exciting
new ventures.

159

I feel safe
in the
rhythm
and flow of
ever-changing
life.

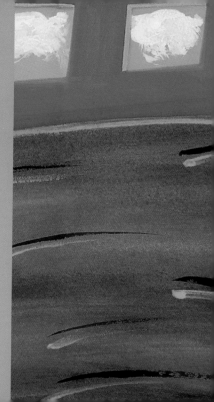

160

The past has no power over me. I know that it is over, and I live solely in the present.

I see my patterns and make changes without embarrassment or guilt.

162

I cross all
bridges with
joy and ease.

163

I experience love wherever I go. Loving people fill my life, and I find myself easily expressing love to others.

164

I am at
peace with
my sexuality.
I embrace
myself with
love and
compassion.

165

I trust the
process of life
to bring me
my highest
good.

I recognize
that awareness
is the first
step in healing
or changing.
I become
more aware
with each
passing day.

167

My thoughts
are creative.
I constantly
have new
insights and
new ways of
looking at my
world.

168

The answers
within me
come to my
awareness
with ease.

169

I respect my father for his love, his good judgment, and for just being who he is.

170

I know that
the point of
power is
always in
the present
moment.

171

I am willing to grow and change. Every moment presents a wonderful new opportunity to become more of who I am.

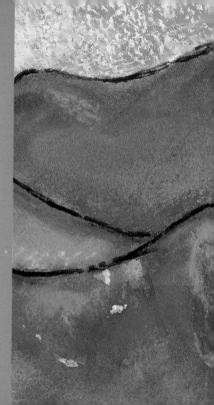

172

I am totally adequate at all times. I accept myself and create peace in my mind and heart.

173

No job is
beneath me
or above me.
If something
needs doing,
I do it.

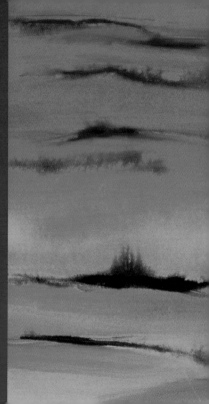

174

I take full
responsibility
for every
aspect of my
life.

175

I love my body. **Every** year I feel more relaxed and more attractive.

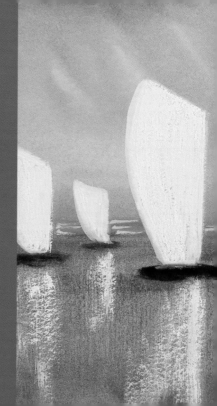

176

I deserve the best, and I accept it now. All my needs and desires are met before I even ask.

177

I express
my creativity
openly and
freely.

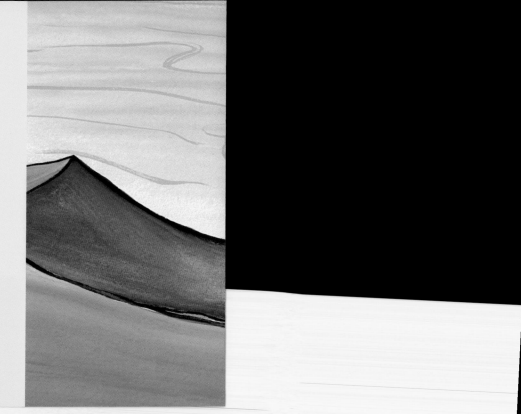

178

I am willing to release the pattern in me that is creating any negative condition in my life.

179

All that I
desire, I
receive. I am
fulfilled in
all areas of
my life.

180

I am my
best friend.
I love what
I see in me.

181

I allow
change to
occur without
resistance
or fear.
I am free.

182

I am perfect

just as I am.

183

I give myself
permission to
be all that
I can be, and
I deserve the
very best
in life.

184

I am totally free to choose thoughts of joy. It is my Divine right to do so.

185

I embrace my
entire being
with love and
compassion.

186

I love who
I am, and
reward
myself with
thoughts of
praise.

187

I release the need to blame anyone. I accept the people around me as they are.

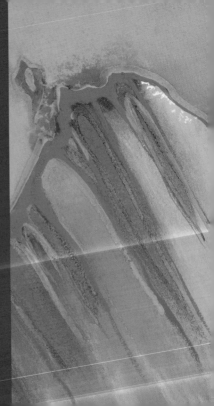

188

This is a
new day.
I am a
new me.

189

Everything
in my life
happens in
the perfect
space-time
sequence.

Abundance is drawn to my every action. I am a magnet for Divine prosperity.

191

I turn every
experience
into an
opportunity.

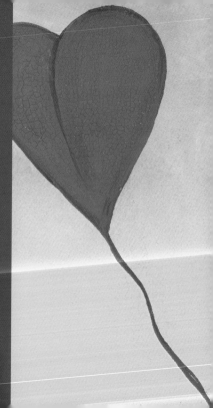

192

It is safe
for me to
be flexible
enough to
see others'
viewpoints.

193

I have the
Divine right
to be fulfilled
in all areas
of life. I
am worthy
of success.

194

I easily
flow with
new
experiences
and new
opportunities.

I easily and comfortably release that which I no longer need.

196

I am
totally and
completely
supported by
the Universe.

My body
uses relaxation
as a time to
repair and
rejuvenate
itself. The
more I relax,
the healthier
I am.

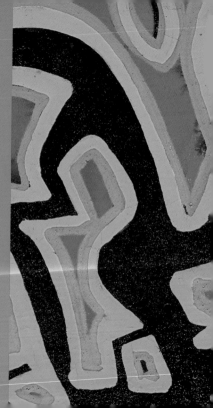

198

I speak up
for myself
with ease. I
am intelligent
and powerful.

199

Every experience I have leads me to a greater understanding of my purpose on Earth.

200

My income
is constantly
increasing.

201

Every
problem has
a solution.
Learning is
easy and fun
for me.

202

I am willing
to grow up
and deal with
my feelings.

203

Other people
respect me
because
I respect
myself.

204

Only that which I no longer need leaves my life. Everything that surrounds me serves a purpose.

205

I look
forward with
enthusiasm
to the
adventures
of the day.

206

I expect life
to be safe
and joyous.
I attract all
that is good.

207

My heart
is open.
I speak
with loving
words.

208

I rejoice in
what I have,
and I know
that fresh,
new experi-
ences are
always ahead
of me.

209

I have unlimited choices about what I can think. My mind feels free and light.

210

I am now
willing to
see my own
beauty and
magnificence.

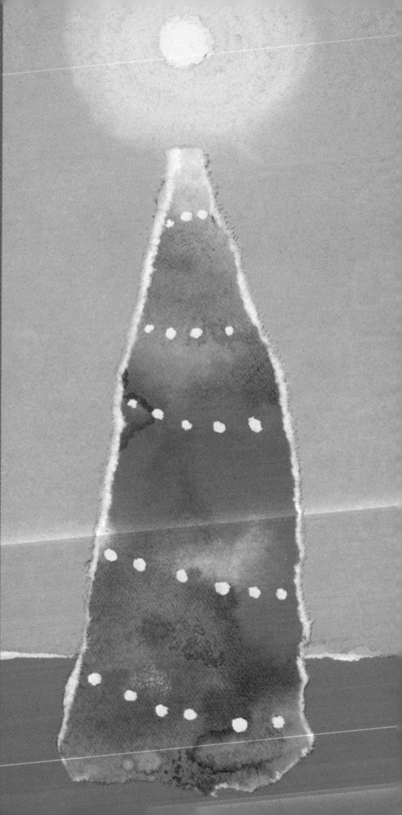

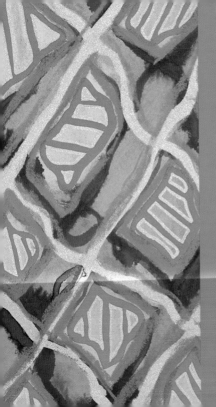

211

I am totally
adequate
for all
situations.

212

I now choose
to support
myself in
loving, joyous
ways.

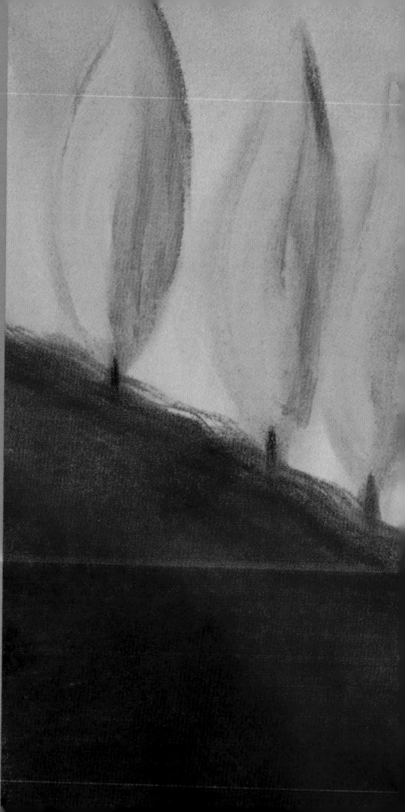

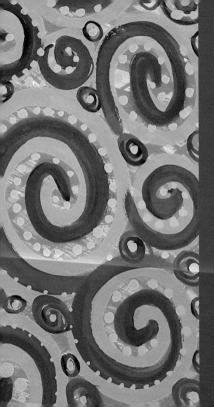

213

I listen
with love to
my body's
messages. My
body is the
picture of
total health.

214

I laugh at life (and at myself), and choose not to be offended by anyone or anything.

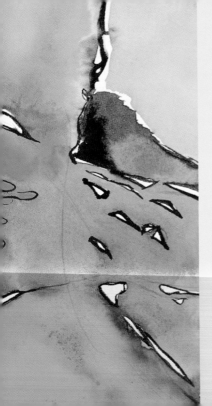

215

I handle
all my
experiences
with wisdom,
love, and ease.

216

I am open
and receptive
to new
avenues
of income.

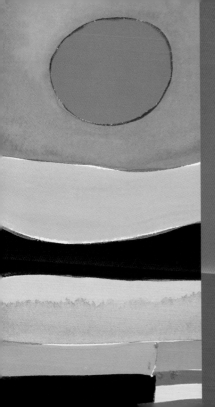

217

I am
enthusiastic
about life. I
am filled
with energy
and optimism.

Every
moment
presents a
wonderful
new
opportunity to
become more
of who I am.

219

I now
choose to
release all
hurt and
resentment.

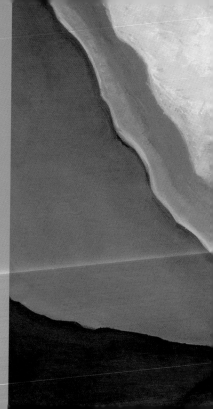

220

I see only
harmony
around me
at all times.
I am always
safe and
secure.

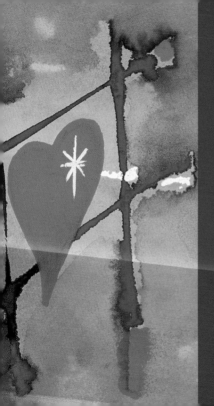

221

I experience
love wherever
I go.

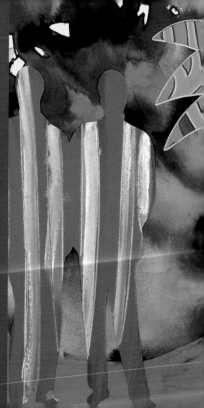

222

Compliments
are gifts of
prosperity. I
accept them
graciously.

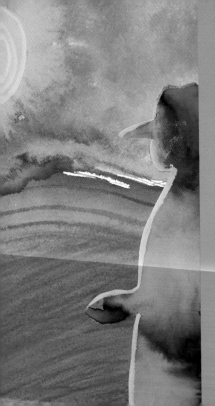

223

I am at home

in my body.

I think positive
thoughts,
because every
cell within my
body responds
to every
thought I think
and every word
I speak.

225

I look within

to find my

treasures.

226

I am aware that what I do not want to change is exactly what I need to change the most.

227

Whatever I
am guided to
do will be a
success.

228

Everyone changes, and I allow change in everyone.

229

I accept myself, and create peace in my mind and heart.

230

Today is a wonderful day. I choose to make it so.

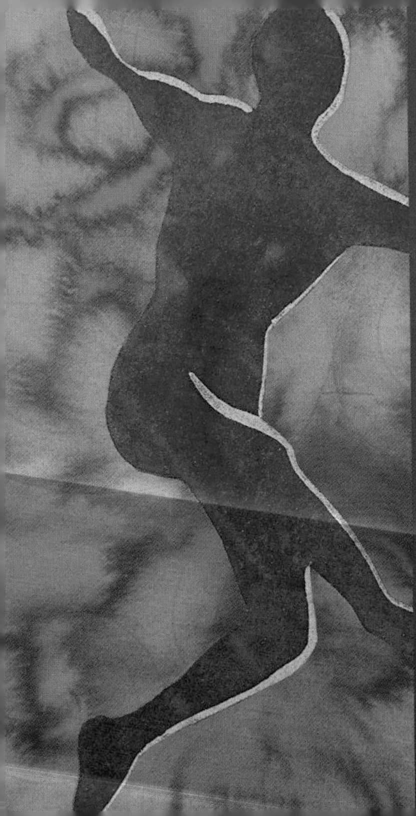

231

I accept
perfect health
as my natural
state of being.

232

My
understanding
is clear, and I
am willing to
change with
the times.

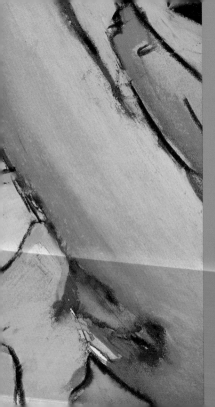

233

I take brisk walks in the sunshine to invigorate my body and soul.

234

My body
wants to be
active and
healthy.
Exercise is
fun for me.

235

I am free
to think
wonderful
thoughts. I
am in control
of my own
mind.

236

Love flows
through my
very being.
It touches
everyone I
meet and
leads me to
greater
compassion.

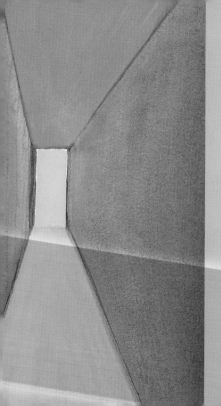

237

**All that I
seek is
already
within me.**

238

I forgive
others, and I
now create
my life in the
way I want
it to be.

239

I move beyond limited human-mind thinking and align myself with the infinite Divine Mind, where all things are possible.

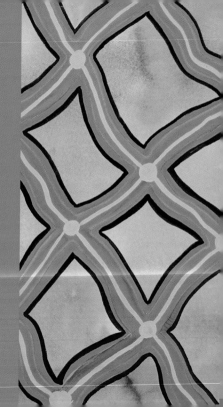

240

I feel
glorious,
dynamic
energy.
I am active
and alive.

241

I rejoice in
new growth.
I leave all
reservations
behind me.

242

It is my birthright to express myself creatively in ways that are deeply fulfilling to me. I have fun today!

243

I rejoice in
what I have,
and I meet
all challenges
with open
arms.

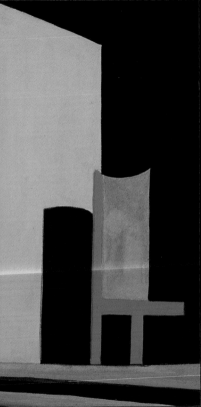

244

I open new
doors to life.
New areas of
loving are
always ahead
of me.

245

I am in the
perfect place
at the perfect
time. I am
always safe.

246

My life is a
party to be
experienced
and shared
with everyone
I know.

247

I work for enjoyment and satisfaction— and not just to earn a living. I use my mind and thoughts to enhance my life.

248

Life
supports me.
It brings
me only
positive
experiences.

249

My inner
quest is
rewarding
and provides
me with
many
answers.

250

I learn my
lessons in life
easily and
effortlessly.

251

Love operates
in all of my
relationships,
from the
most casual
to the most
intimate.

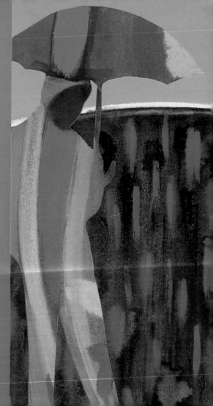

252

My day
begins and
ends with
gratitude and
joy.

253

This planet is
my home. I
take loving
care of the
earth and all
the living
creatures
upon it.

254

I am always
the perfect
age for where
I am in my
life.

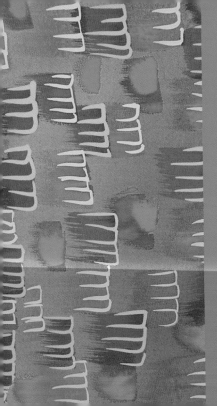

I open my home and welcome guests with music and love. They are like a loving family to me.

256

I am willing
to let go of
old beliefs
that
no longer
serve me.

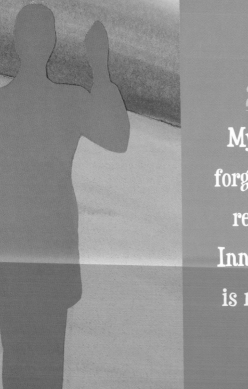

257

My heart
forgives and
releases.
Inner peace
is my goal.

258

Every
experience
I have is
perfect for
my growth.

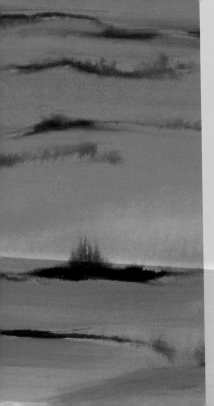

259

I am organized and productive. I am energetic and enjoy getting my life in order.

260

I release all criticism. I go beyond any feelings of not being capable and creative enough.

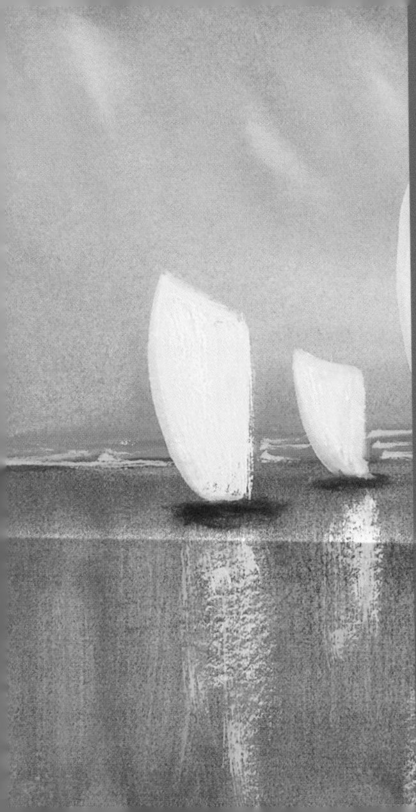

261

I am gentle and kind with myself as I grow and change.

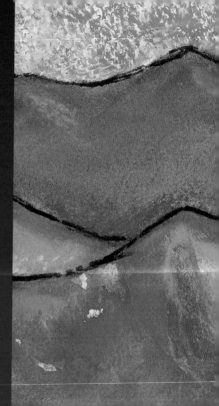

262

I use my
Inner
Wisdom
to run the
business of
my life.

263

The pathway
to love is
forgiveness.
I lovingly
release the
past and turn
my attention
to this
new day.

264

I expand my
boundaries
to encompass
only positive
experiences.

265

Knowing that friends and lovers were once strangers to me, I welcome new people into my life.

266

Life mirrors
my every
thought. As
I keep my
thoughts
positive, life
brings me
only good
experiences.

267

It gives me
joy to take
care of
myself and
others.

268

The Universe
totally
supports
every thought
I choose to
think and
believe.

269

Divine peace
and harmony
surround me
at all times.

270

I release
and let go.
I gladly
give away all
that I no
longer need.

271

My prosperous thoughts create my prosperous world.

272

I rejoice in
my body.
I am glowing
health
personified.

273

I am independent, and I do what I want to do. I try out new ideas. I am a leader today.

274

My life
reflects good,
and only good
is reflected
back at me.
I am the cool,
calm expres-
sion of life.

<u>275</u>

I always
work with
and for
wonderful
people. I love
my job.

276

My mind
and body are
in perfect
balance.
I am
a harmonious
being.

277

I lovingly accept my decisions, knowing that I am free to change.

278

I constantly
have new
insights and
new ways of
looking at the
world.

279

I move
forward with
confidence
and ease,
knowing that
all is well in
my future.

280

I become
more lovable
every day. I
am seen by
others as
a loving,
forgiving
person.

281

I am
responsible
for all of my
experiences.

282

People
respect me
and are very
appreciative
of everything
I do.

283

I radiate
warmth and
love. I am
beautiful,
and everyone
loves me.

284

I awaken to
my golden
opportunities.

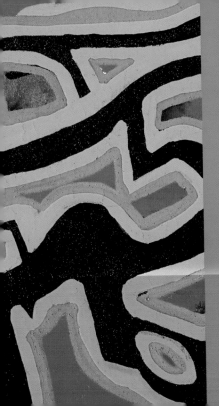

I now attract
new friends
who are
exciting,
loving, caring,
accepting,
funny, and
generous.

286

I rely on
Divine
wisdom and
guidance to
protect me at
all times.

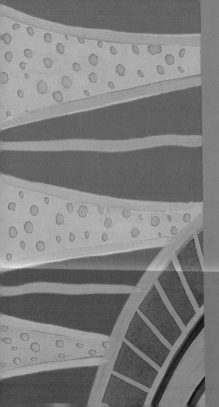

287

I love life!
I look
forward
to every
moment
of it.

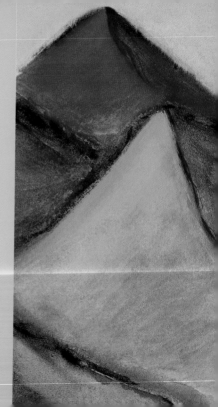

288

Whenever I
have a problem,
I know that
it comes from
my limiting
thought patterns.
I effortlessly
solve my prob-
lems by choosing
positive thoughts.

My home is a
peaceful haven.
I put love in
every corner,
and my home
lovingly
responds with
warmth and
comfort.

290

I express
my emotions
in joyous,
positive ways.

291

I am
unlimited in
my wealth.
All areas of
my life are
abundant and
fulfilling.

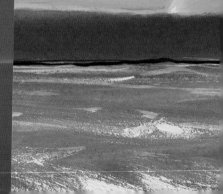

292

I am grateful
for life's
generosity to
me. I am
truly blessed.

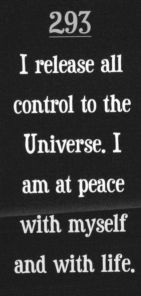

293

I release all
control to the
Universe. I
am at peace
with myself
and with life.

294

I grow beyond my family's limitations and live for myself. It is *my* turn now.

295

I free myself
and everyone
in my life
from old past
hurts.

296

Wellness is the natural state of my body. I believe in perfect health.

297

I am
constantly
moving
forward in
the direction
of my goals.

298

I am as
successful
as I make
up my mind
to be.

299

I respect and
protect my
body because
my health is
important
to me.

300

I open my
heart and
sing the joys
of love.

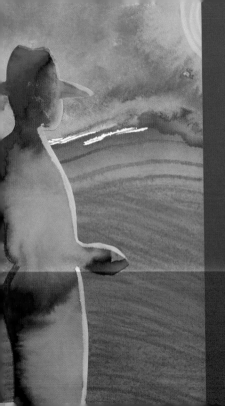

301

Divine peace
and love
surround me
and dwell in
me. I trust
the process
of life.

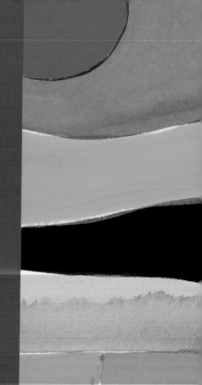

302

I am in total harmony with my environment: the sun, the moon, the wind, the rain, and the earth.

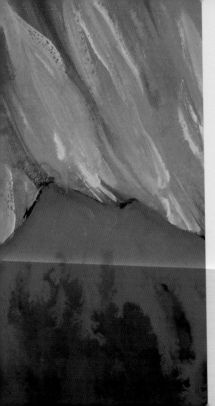

303

I dress
beautifully
every day
because doing
so lifts my
spirits.

304

I create
peacefulness
in my mind.
I trust
my inner
wisdom.

305

Every
bridge
I cross
brings me
to a higher
level of
fulfillment.

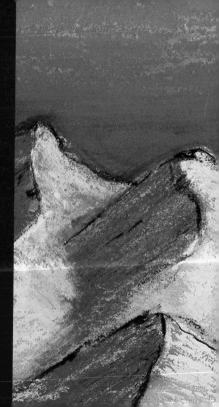

306

I choose
harmony
and loving
communication
wherever
I am.

307

I appreciate
all that I do.
I am the most
important
person in
my life.

308

Every person, place, and thing on this planet is interconnected with love. I am at home in the Universe.

309

We are all
doing the
best we can
with the
understanding,
knowledge,
and awareness
we have.

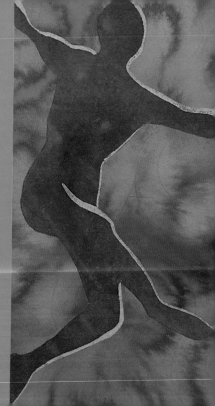

310

I joyfully
keep my inner
child safe at
the center of
my being. I
love and
cherish my
inner child.

311

Every
moment is
a new
beginning.
My life is
so sweet.

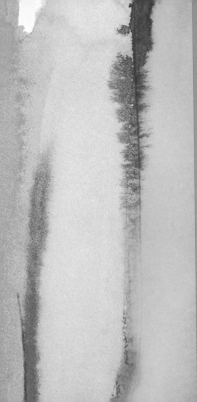

313

With my
loving attitude,
I help to create
a world where
it is safe for
us to love
each other.

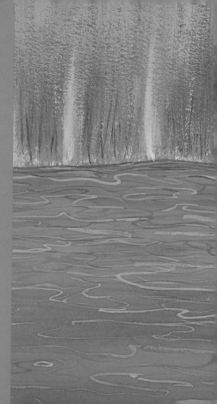

314

Peace begins
with me. The
more peaceful I
am inside, the
more peace I
have to share
with others.
World peace
really does begin
with me.

315

I follow my
inner star. I
am a shining
example of
love and light.

316

I take the
things I
think are
"wrong"
about me and
turn them
into positive
affirmations.

317

I inhale the precious breath of life; and I allow my body, mind, and emotions to relax.

318

I handle my
own life with
joy and ease.

319

I am proud
that I can
easily adapt
to the ebb
and flow of
my life.

320

I am gentle, kind, and patient with myself. Those around me reflect this tender care.

321

I give love
to all the
animals who
come into my
life. They are
gifts from the
Universe.

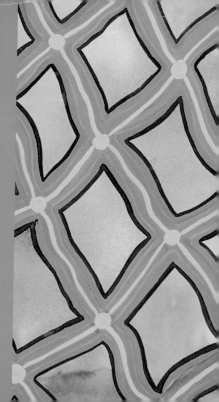

322

My body is always work- ing toward optimal health. I am happy and healthy.

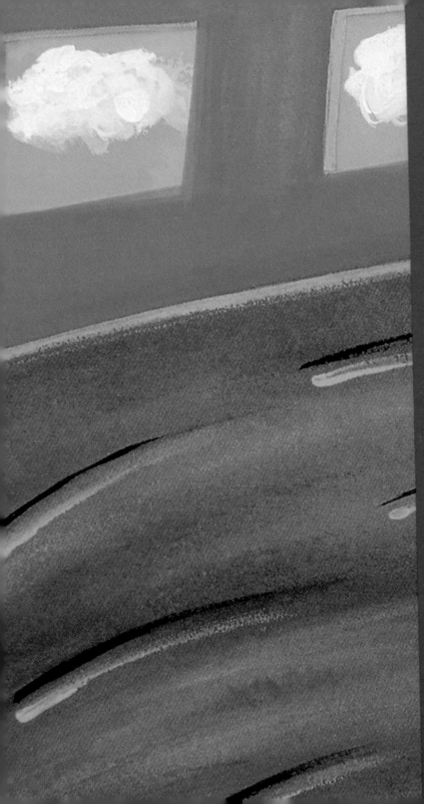

323

Today is the
future I
created
yesterday.

324

I rejoice in
the knowl-
edge that
I have the
power of my
own mind to
use in any
way I choose.

<u>325</u>

Everything
in my life
works now
and forever-
more.

326

My thinking
is peaceful,
calm, and
centered.

327

I am thankful for all the days of my life that I have lived so far. I am also thankful for all the days I have yet to live. Life is so good.

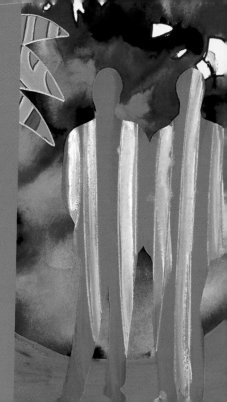

328

My good
comes from
everywhere
and everyone
and every-
thing.

329

The gateways
to wisdom and
knowledge are
always open
to me.

330

I constantly
have new
insights.
My future
is glorious.

331

Whenever
I travel, I
am protected
and safe. I
always have
an enjoyable
time.

332

I take time today to bask in the love and light of my life.
What a glorious day!

333

Forgiving
makes me
feel free
and light.
I forgive
everyone,
including
myself.

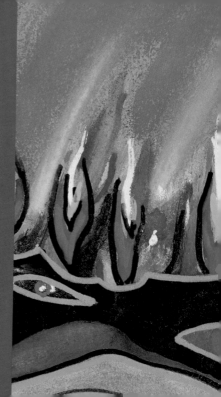

334

I am guided throughout this day to make all the right choices. I only desire that which is for my highest good.

335

I find joy and
appreciation
in everything
I say and do.

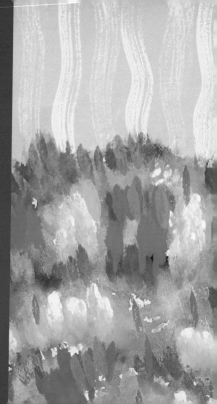

336

The joy in
my life is
overflowing.
My life gets
better all
the time.

I am open
and receptive
to all the
good and
abundance in
the Universe.

338

I create
my own
experiences.
As I love and
approve of
myself and
others, my life
gets better
and better.

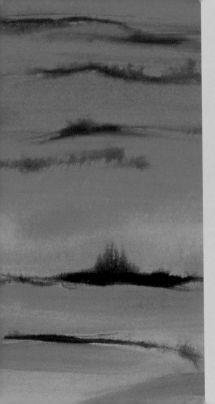

339

All of my
friends
understand
my needs. I
have many
friends who
love me.

340

My mind is a
tool that I can
choose to use
in any way
I wish.

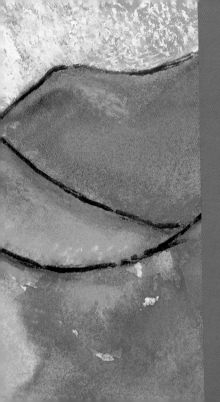

341

I make time
to do the
things that I
enjoy. I get
out and expe-
rience life in
a new way.

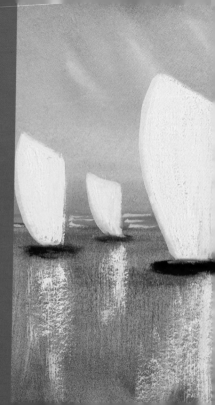

342

**All my needs
and desires
are met
before I even
ask. All
is well in
my world.**

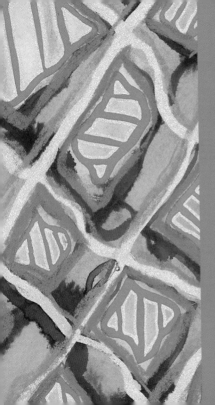

343

Joyous new
ideas are
circulating
freely
within me.

344

I know that before others will love me, I have to love myself. My self-love begins now.

345

I respect all
the members
of my family,
and they,
in turn,
respect me.

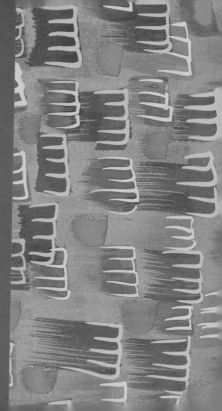

346

I view all experiences as opportunities for me to learn and grow.

347

I see myself as beautiful, lovable, and appreciated. I am proud to be me.

348

I deserve to
enjoy life. I
ask for what
I want, and
I accept it
with joy
and pleasure.

349

My home
fulfills all my
needs and
desires. I fill
my home
with love.

350

I now free myself from destructive fears and doubts.

351

People love

to be with

me, and I

love to be

with people.

352

It is my birthright to share in the abundance and prosperity of this world.

353

I only speak
positively
about those in
my world.
Negativity has
no part in
my life.

354

Difficulties
no longer
burden me.
I easily
solve all
problems.

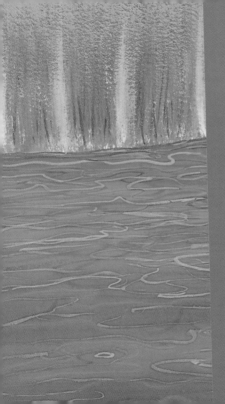

355

I am an open
channel for
creative ideas.

356

I am capable and organized. My efficiency is more than ample to get any job done.

357

I am
empowered
and confident.
I hold my
head up high.

358

A smiling face and joyful, loving words are the best presents I can share with everyone I know.

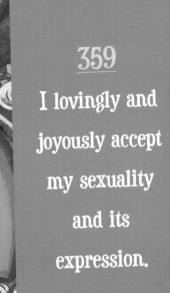

359

I lovingly and
joyously accept
my sexuality
and its
expression.

360

I treat my partner with love and respect, and receive the same in return.

361

I am willing
to release all
patterns of
criticism.

362

I am a decisive and productive person. I follow through with tasks that I start and make no excuses.

363

I read books
that enrich
my soul and
give me food
for thought.
There is
always more
to learn.

364

The love
from my
heart flows
joyously
through my
body.

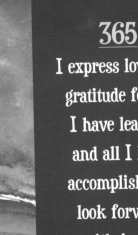

365

I express love and gratitude for all I have learned and all I have accomplished. I look forward with joyous anticipation to each new day of my life. All is well in my world!

Also by Louise Hay

BOOKS/KITS

All Is Well (with Mona Lisa Schulz, M.D., Ph.D.)

Colors & Numbers

Empowering Women

Everyday Positive Thinking

Experience Your Good Now! (book-with-CD)

A Garden of Thoughts: My Affirmation Journal

Gratitude: A Way of Life (Louise & Friends)

Heal Your Body

Heal Your Body A–Z

Heart Thoughts (also available in a gift edition)

I Can Do It® (book-with-CD)

Inner Wisdom

Letters to Louise

Life! Reflections on Your Journey

Love Your Body

Love Yourself, Heal Your Life Workbook

Meditations to Heal Your Life (also available in a gift edition)

Modern-Day Miracles (Louise & Friends)

The Power Is Within You

The Present Moment

The Times of Our Lives (Louise & Friends)

You Can Create an Exceptional Life (with Cheryl Richardson)

You Can Heal Your Heart (with David Kessler)

You Can Heal Your Life (also available in a gift edition)

You Can Heal Your Life Affirmation Kit

You Can Heal Your Life Companion Book

FOR CHILDREN

The Adventures of Lulu

I Think, I Am! (with Kristina Tracy)

Lulu and the Ant: A

Message of Love

Lulu and the Dark: Conquering Fears

Lulu and Willy the Duck: Learning Mirror Work

CD PROGRAMS

All Is Well (audio book)

Anger Releasing

Cancer

Change and Transition

Dissolving Barriers

Embracing Change

The Empowering Women Gift Collection

Feeling Fine Affirmations

Forgiveness/Loving the Inner Child

How to Love Yourself

Meditations for Personal Healing

Meditations to Heal Your Life (audio book)

Morning and Evening Meditations

101 Power Thoughts

Overcoming Fears

The Power Is Within You (audio book)

The Power of Your Spoken Word

Receiving Prosperity

Self-Esteem Affirmations (subliminal)

Self-Healing

Stress-Free (subliminal)

Totality of Possibilities

What I Believe and Deep Relaxation

You Can Heal Your Life (audio book)

You Can Heal Your Life Study Course

Your Thoughts Create Your Life

DVDs

Receiving Prosperity

You Can Heal Your Life Study Course

You Can Heal Your Life, THE MOVIE (also available in an expanded edition)

You Can Trust Your Life (with Cheryl Richardson)

CARD DECKS

Healthy Body Cards

I Can Do It® Cards

I Can Do It® Cards . . . for Creativity, Forgiveness, Health, Job Success, Wealth, Romance

Power Thought Cards

Power Thoughts for Teens

Power Thought Sticky Cards

Wisdom Cards

CALENDAR

I Can Do It® Calendar (for each individual year)

and

THE ESSENTIAL LOUISE HAY COLLECTION

(comprising *You Can Heal Your Life, Heal Your Body,* and *The Power Is Within You* in a single volume)

All of the above are available at your local bookstore, or may be ordered by visiting:

Hay House USA:
www.hayhouse.com®

Hay House Australia:
www.hayhouse.com.au

Hay House UK:
www.hayhouse.co.uk

Hay House South Africa:
www.hayhouse.co.za

Hay House India:
www.hayhouse.co.in

Louise's websites:
www.LouiseHay.com®

and

www.HealYourLife.com®

About Louise Hay

Louise Hay is a metaphysical lecturer and teacher and the best-selling author of numerous books, including *You Can Heal Your Life* and *I Can Do It*®. Her works have been translated into 29 different languages in 35 countries throughout the world. For more than 30 years, Louise has assisted millions of people in discovering and using the full potential of their own creative powers for personal growth and self-healing. Louise is the founder and chairman of Hay House, Inc., a publishing company that disseminates books, audios, and videos that contribute to the healing of the planet. Websites: www.LouiseHay.com or www.HealYourLife.com

To receive a free issue of *The Louise Hay Newsletter*, please call Hay House at: 800-654-5126.

Titles of Related Interest by Other Hay House Authors

Books

Everything I've Ever Done That Worked, by Lesley Garner
The Gift of Peace, by Ben Stein
Staying on the Path, by Dr. Wayne W. Dyer
Sylvia Browne's Lessons for Life, by Sylvia Browne
Three Keys to Self-Empowerment, by Stuart Wilde
Zest for Life, by Dawn Breslin

Card Decks

Attitude Is Everything Cards, by Keith D. Harrell
Empowerment Cards for Inspired Living, by Tavis Smiley
Healthy Living Cards, by the Staff at Canyon Ranch
The Language of Letting Go Cards, by Melody Beattie
The Power of Intention Cards, by Dr. Wayne W. Dyer
The Voice of Knowledge Cards, by DON Miguel Ruiz

All of the above are available at your local bookstore,
or may be ordered by visiting:
Hay House USA: **www.hayhouse.com**®
Hay House Australia: **www.hayhouse.com.au**
Hay House UK: **www.hayhouse.co.uk**
Hay House South Africa: **www.hayhouse.co.za**
Hay House India: **www.hayhouse.co.in**

We hope you enjoyed this Hay House Lifestyles book.
If you would like to receive our online catalog featuring additional
Hay House books and products, or if you would like information
about the Hay Foundation or a free copy of *The Louise Hay
Newsletter*, please contact:

Hay House, Inc., P.O. Box 5100, Carlsbad, CA 92018-5100

(760) 431-7695 or (800) 654-5126
(760) 431-6948 (fax) or (800) 650-5115 (fax)
www.hayhouse.com®

Published and distributed in Australia by:
Hay House Australia Pty. Ltd., 18/36 Ralph St., Alexandria NSW 2015
Phone: 612-9669-4299 • *Fax:* 612-9669-4144 • www.hayhouse.com.au

Published and distributed in the United Kingdom by:
Hay House UK, Ltd., Astley House, 33 Notting Hill Gate,
London W11 3JQ • *Phone:* 44-20-3675-2450
Fax: 44-20-3675-2451 • www.hayhouse.co.uk

Published and distributed in the Republic of South Africa by:
Hay House SA (Pty), Ltd., P.O. Box 990, Witkoppen 2068 • *Phone/Fax:*
27-11-467-8904 • info@hayhouse.co.za • www.hayhouse.co.za

Published in India by:
Hay House Publishers India, Muskaan Complex, Plot No. 3, B-2,
Vasant Kunj, New Delhi 110 070 • *Phone:* 91-11-4176-1620
Fax: 91-11-4176-1630 • www.hayhouse.co.in

Distributed in Canada by:
Raincoast Books, 2440 Viking Way, Richmond, B.C. V6V 1N2
Phone: 1-800-663-5714 • *Fax:* 1-800-565-3770 • www.raincoast.com